THE TEEN ENTREPRENEURSHIP
TEXTBOOK

EVERYTHING I WISH I WAS TAUGHT TO SUCCEED IN THE BUSINESS WORLD AS A YOUNG ENTREPRENEUR.

D1528305

Table of Contents:

The information provided in this book is for informational purposes only and is not intended to be a source of advice or credit analysis with respect to the material presented. The information and/or documents contained in this book do not constitute legal or financial advice and should never be used without first consulting with a financial professional to determine what may be best for your individual needs.

The publisher and the author do not make any guarantee or other promise as to any results that may be obtained from using the content of this book. You should never make any investment decision without first consulting with your own financial advisor and conducting your own research and due diligence. To the maximum extent permitted by law, the publisher and the author disclaim any and all liability in the event any information, commentary, analysis, opinions, advice and/or recommendations contained in this book prove to be inaccurate, incomplete or unreliable, or result in any investment or other losses.

Content contained or made available through this book is not intended to and does not constitute legal advice or investment advice and no attorney-client relationship is formed. The publisher and the author are providing this book and its contents on an "as is" basis. Your use of the information in this book is at your own risk.

Hey,

I'm Brendan.

Although I am no longer a teen entrepreneur I was in your shoes just a few years ago. Before I dive into entrepreneurship itself - I think it's important for you to know who I am and why I chose to write this book.

My name is Brendan Cox and I'm 22 years of age at the time of writing this. I have had a passion for making money since an extremely young age. From setting up lemonade stands as a kid to buying and selling sneakers as a teenager to now, where I build and sell real companies. My passion for entrepreneurship has been with me since a very young age and it continues to drive me today.

While many people choose to go to college and follow a traditional path, I decided to take a different route. I went to college for one year, but then I made the decision to drop out and pursue entrepreneurship. I felt that the traditional path wasn't right for me and that I would be better able to follow my passions and achieve my goals through entrepreneurship.

As I look back on my 13 years of formal education, I can't help but feel disappointed by the lack of practical, real-world skills and knowledge that I was taught. It seems that much of what I learned in school was disconnected from the everyday challenges and opportunities that I have faced as an adult. While I value the importance of a solid foundation in core subjects, I believe that it is equally important for students to learn skills that are relevant and applicable to the modern world.

In this book, I share the insights and lessons that I have learned through my own experiences and self-directed learning. These are the things that I wish I had been taught in school, but instead I had to discover and learn them on my own. With this book, I hope to share my knowledge and help others navigate some of the challenges and obstacles that I faced when pursuing the exciting world of entrepreneurship at such a young age.

Part I: Intro

CHAPTER 1

Exploring the World of Entrepreneurship

"Entrepreneurship is about turning what excites you in life into capital so that you can do more of it and move forward with it." – Richard Branson

If you're reading this, you're probably a young person with big dreams of making it big in the business world. You're driven, ambitious, and eager to turn your ideas into reality. Before we get into the interesting stuff, it's important to define some key terms that will be useful for you to understand:

- Entrepreneurship: The process of creating or starting a new business venture in order to make a profit by identifying a need and developing a product or service to meet that need. It encompasses the act of being an entrepreneur, the mindset of an entrepreneur, and the various strategies and methods used to start and grow a business.

- Entrepreneur: An individual who starts, organizes, and manages a new business venture, typically with the goal of making a profit by identifying a need and developing a product or service to meet that need. Entrepreneurs are known for their ability to identify opportunities and take risks to turn their ideas into successful businesses.

Entrepreneurship is the process of starting and running a business, typically involving the creation of a new product or service and the assumption of taking on financial risks in order to do so. It involves identifying a market opportunity, developing a business plan, and taking the necessary steps to bring the business to fruition. You, the entrepreneur, are an individual who takes on this process and is willing to take risks in order to turn your ideas into reality. You are self-motivated, innovative, and driven by a desire to create something new and successful.

Entrepreneurship can take many forms, and it is not limited to traditional notions of starting a brick and mortar business. It can also involve creating and selling products or services online, developing a software or app, or even becoming an influencer on social media. The key aspect of entrepreneurship is the creation and growth of a new business venture.

Entrepreneurship requires a wide range of skills and knowledge, including business planning, marketing, financial management, and leadership. It can be a challenging and rewarding career path, but it also comes with a certain level of risk and uncertainty. Successful entrepreneurs are able to identify opportunities, develop and execute a plan, and adapt to changing circumstances in order to achieve their goals. They are able to take calculated risks, learn from their mistakes, and overcome challenges. Overall, entrepreneurship is about creating value, taking control of your career, and making a positive impact on the world.

In this section, we'll be taking a closer look at the basics of entrepreneurship and what it takes to succeed as a young entrepreneur. By the end of this section, you should have a solid foundation of key principles and be well on your way to turning your dreams into a reality.

CHAPTER 2

The Ups and Downs of Being Your Own Boss

"Entrepreneurship is living a few years of life like most people won't, so that you can spend the rest of your life like most people can't." — Anonymous

Entrepreneurship can be a rewarding and fulfilling career path, but it is not without its challenges and risks. It's important to carefully consider both the pros and cons of this career before making a decision about whether it's the right path for you.

On the plus side, entrepreneurship offers the opportunity to be your own boss and build a business that aligns with your passions and values. It can also be highly lucrative, with the potential to earn significantly more than you might in a traditional job. Entrepreneurship also allows for a greater degree of flexibility and control over your career, allowing you to set your own schedule and priorities.

However, as mentioned, entrepreneurship also comes with a number of risks and challenges. Starting and growing a business can be a long and difficult process, and there is no guarantee of success. It can be financially risky, as entrepreneurs often have to invest a significant amount of their own money into their businesses to get started. There is also a lot of hard work and long hours involved, as entrepreneurs are responsible for every aspect of their business. Additionally, there is a level of uncertainty and insecurity that comes attached to this career path, as there is no guarantee of a steady income or job security.

Additionally, entrepreneurship can be a lonely and isolating experience at times, as you may not have the support and camaraderie of a traditional workplace. It can also be difficult to find and retain good employees, as you may not have the resources or reputation of a larger company. Finally, there may be legal and regulatory hurdles to overcome, such as obtaining necessary licenses and permits, and complying with various laws and regulations.

Despite these challenges, many entrepreneurs find the rewards of building their own business to be well worth the effort. If you are willing to take the risk and put in the hard work, entrepreneurship can be a fulfilling and rewarding career path that allows you to make a difference in the world and achieve financial success on your own terms.

Pros of being an entrepreneur:	Cons of being an entrepreneur:
• Ability to be your own boss and make your own decisions • Potential to earn more money than you would as an employee • Greater flexibility and control over your career • Opportunity to build a business that aligns with your passions and values • Ability to create a positive impact on the world	• Higher risk and uncertainty compared to being an employee • Long hours and hard work required to start and grow a business • Financial risk, as entrepreneurs often have to invest a significant amount of their own money into their businesses • Isolation and lack of support compared to working in a traditional workplace • Difficulty finding and retaining good employees • Legal and regulatory hurdles to overcome
Pros of being an employee:	Cons of being an employee:
• Steady income and job security	Limited control over your career and job duties

• Support and resources of a larger company • Ability to focus on a specific role or task, rather than managing every aspect of a business • Opportunity to learn from and work with experienced professionals • Work-life balance may be easier to maintain	Dependence on someone else for employment and decision-making Limited opportunity to earn more money or make a significant impact Limited flexibility in terms of schedule and location

It's important to carefully consider the pros and cons of entrepreneurship and ask yourself some key questions before making a decision about whether it's the right path for you. Here are some questions that you may want to consider:

- Are you self-motivated and able to work independently?

- Are you comfortable with risk and uncertainty?

- Do you have a clear vision and business plan?

- Do you have the necessary skills and knowledge to succeed as an entrepreneur?

- Do you have a support network in place, including advisors, mentors, and potential partners or employees?

- Are you willing to put in the hard work and long hours required to start and grow a business?

- Do you have the financial resources to invest in your business and support yourself during the start-up phase?

- Do you have the resilience and adaptability to overcome challenges and setbacks?

Asking yourself these important questions can help you determine whether entrepreneurship is the right fit for you and your goals. It's important to be honest with yourself and realistic about the challenges and risks involved, as well as the potential rewards.

CHAPTER 3

The Basics of Grammar for Business Owners

*"The defining factor for success is never resources,
but resourcefulness." - Anthony Robbins*

Effective communication is an essential skill for any entrepreneur, and having a strong understanding of business terminology is an important part of this. While many books may cover the basics, it can be helpful to have a list of key terms and concepts to get familiar with.

Here are 50 key terms that are important to know when starting your first business:

1. Assets: Refer to anything of value that a company or an individual owns, such as property, equipment, cash, and investments. They can be tangible (physical) or intangible (non-physical).

2. Business plan: A document that outlines a company's goals, strategies, and projected financial performance. It is used to secure

funding, attract investors, and guide a company's operations.

3. Capital: Refers to the money or assets that a company or an individual has available to invest in a business or other venture. It can also refer to the total value of a company's assets minus its liabilities.

4. Cashflow: The flow of money into and out of a business or individual's bank account. It is the difference between the amount of cash coming in (revenue) and going out (expenses) over a specific period of time.

5. Competition: Refers to the presence of other businesses or individuals offering similar products or services in the same market. It can also refer to the rivalry between companies or individuals to gain market share or customers.

6. Copyright: A legal right that gives creators of original works (such as books, music, and software) exclusive rights to reproduce and distribute their work for a certain period of time.

7. Crowdfunding: A method of raising money for a project or business venture through small contributions from a large number of people, typically via the internet.

8. Debt: Money that is borrowed and must be repaid, often with interest. It can refer to money owed by a company or individual to a lender or creditor.

9. Elevator pitch: A brief, persuasive speech used to spark interest in a product, service, or idea. The name comes from the idea that it should be short enough to deliver during a brief elevator ride.

10. Fixed costs: Expenses that a business must pay regardless of the level of production or sales. Examples include rent, salaries, and insurance. They do not change with the level of production.

11. Forecast: Forecast is an estimate or prediction of future events or conditions, often used in business to predict financial performance or market trends.

12. Founder: The person or group of people who establish a business or organization.

13. Gross profit: A measure of a company's financial performance, calculated as revenue minus the cost of goods sold. It represents the amount of revenue that remains after accounting for the direct costs associated with producing and selling a product or service.

14. Innovation: Refers to the introduction of new or improved products, processes, or ideas. It is the process of creating new or improved products, processes, and ideas to meet the needs of customers or solve problems.

15. Intrapreneurship: The process of creating new products, services, or businesses within an existing organization. It is a way for employees to act like entrepreneurs within the company.

16. Investor: A person or organization that puts money into a business or project with the expectation of making a profit.

17. Key performance indicator (KPI): A metric used to measure the success of a business or a specific aspect of it. It can be financial, such as revenue growth, or non-financial, such as customer satisfaction.

18. Launch: Refers to the introduction of a new product, service, or business to the market.

19. Logo: A graphic design or symbol that represents a company, organization, or brand.

20. Margin: A measure of profitability, often expressed as a percentage of revenue. It is calculated by subtracting the cost of goods sold from revenue and dividing the result by revenue. It can also be used to refer to the difference between the selling price and cost of a product or service.

21. Market analysis: A study of a specific market, including its size, growth, trends, and competitive environment. It is a critical component of a business plan, used to identify and evaluate potential opportunities, as well as assess the potential success of a product or service.

22. Mentor: An experienced and trusted advisor who provides guidance, advice, and support to help someone develop their skills and knowledge.

23. Merger: The combination of two or more companies into a single entity. This can be done

through a merger of equals or an acquisition, where one company is absorbed by another.

24. Negotiate: Means to discuss and reach an agreement with another party on the terms of a deal or transaction. It is the process of reaching a mutually beneficial agreement.

25. Net profit: A measure of a company's financial performance, calculated as revenue minus expenses. It represents the amount of money a company has left over after all its costs and expenses have been paid.

26. Networking: The process of building and maintaining professional relationships. It is the act of connecting with other people to share information, resources, and opportunities.

27. Objectives: Specific, measurable goals that a company or individual hopes to achieve. They are used to guide decision-making and measure progress towards a desired outcome.

28. Outsourcing: The process of hiring a third-party company or individual to perform a specific task or service, rather than doing it in-house.

29. Patent: A legal right granted to inventors for a certain period of time, giving them exclusive rights to make, use, and sell an invention.

30. Pitch: A presentation or proposal, typically used to persuade someone to invest in a business, product, or idea. It is a summary of the key points of a business plan or proposal, presented in a clear and compelling way.

31. Proof of concept: A demonstration or prototype of a proposed product or service, used to test its feasibility and potential value.

32. Revenue: The income generated by a business or organization, typically from the sale of goods or services.

33. Risk: The possibility of loss or injury, or the likelihood of an event occurring that could negatively impact an investment or business.

34. ROI (Return on Investment): The amount of profit or loss generated on an investment, usually expressed as a percentage of the initial investment.

35. Scale: The size or level of something, such as the degree of growth or expansion of a business or market.

36. SEO (Search Engine Optimization): The process of optimizing a website or online content to improve its visibility and ranking on search engines, such as Google.

37. Side hustle: A business or activity undertaken in addition to one's primary job, typically as a way to earn extra money or gain experience.

38. Start-up: A new business venture, typically in the early stages of development and operation.

39. Strategic alliance: A partnership or collaboration between two or more organizations, typically formed to achieve a specific goal or gain a competitive advantage.

40. Tagline: A short phrase or slogan that serves as a memorable and defining statement for a business, product, or service.

41. Target market: The specific group of consumers that a business or organization aims to sell its products or services to.

42. Traction: The level of progress or success that a business or product has achieved, typically measured by metrics such as revenue, customer acquisition, or market share.

43. Trademark: A legally protected symbol, phrase, or design that is used to identify and distinguish a product or service from those of other companies.

44. Trademark infringement: The unauthorized use of a trademark by a company or individual, which can lead to legal action.

45. Valuation: The process of determining the monetary worth of a business, asset, or investment.

46. Variable costs: Costs that change in relation to the level of production or sales, such as the cost of raw materials or labor.

47. Venture capital: Investment funding provided to start-up companies with high growth potential.

48. Vision: A statement or idea that describes the long-term aspirations of a company or organization.

49. Wantrepreneur: A term used to describe someone who talks about starting a business, but never actually takes action to do so.

50. Intellectual property (IP): Legal rights that protect creations of the mind such as inventions, literary and artistic works, and symbols, names, images, and designs used in commerce. It includes trademarks, patents, copyrights, trade secrets and industrial design rights.

Part II: Concept

CHAPTER 4

The Birth of a Great Idea

"The best way to predict the future is to invent it." -
Alan Kay

Coming up with a business idea can be a challenging and exciting process. It requires creativity, innovation, and a deep understanding of the market and your target audience. However, with the right approach, you can come up with a business idea that not only addresses a need or problem in the market, but also aligns with your passions and values.

The first step in coming up with a business idea is to identify what you are passionate about. This may be a hobby, a cause, a talent, or something else entirely. When you face challenges and setbacks in the early stages of starting a business, it's your passion that will drive your motivation and commitment to keep going. It really is important to choose a business idea that you are genuinely excited about, as this will help to sustain you through the ups and downs of entrepreneurship.

Everyone has interests and causes that they care deeply about, but it can be challenging to recognize them as passions. If you're having trouble identifying your own passion, consider reflecting on the following questions:

1. What are the things that I am naturally drawn to or interested in?

2. What activities do I enjoy doing in my free time?

3. What topics or subjects do I find myself constantly learning or reading about?

4. What causes or issues am I passionate about?

5. What are my strengths and talents?

6. What are my values and what is important to me?

7. How do I want to make a difference or contribution to the world?

8. What kind of work environment do I thrive in?

9. What are my long-term goals and aspirations?

10. What kind of lifestyle do I want to have and how does my passion align with that?

Once you have identified your passion, you can start to think about how you can turn it into a business idea. This may involve identifying a problem or need in the market that your passion can help to solve, or finding a way to bring it to a wider audience. To come up with a business idea based on something you truly care about, it can be helpful to start by brainstorming and jotting down as many ideas as you can. Don't worry about filtering your ideas or being too critical at this stage – the goal is simply to get as many ideas as possible on paper.

Once you have a long list of ideas, you can start to narrow it down by considering things like market demand, competition, and feasibility. It's also important to do some research and validate your business idea. This could require talking to potential customers or clients, conducting market research, or seeking the advice of industry experts. By gathering as much information as possible, you can better understand the potential of your business idea and make informed decisions about whether it is worth pursuing or not.

As you develop your idea, it's important to be open to feedback and willing to pivot if necessary. Entrepreneurship is all about iteration and learning from your mistakes, so don't be afraid to try something new or make changes to your business idea if it's not working. With persistence and determination, you can turn your passion into a successful business.

CHAPTER 5

Standing Out in a Crowded Market

"My advice for an entrepreneur just starting out is to differentiate yourself. Why are you different? What's important about you? Why does the customer need you?" - Sara Blakely

Differentiating yourself in the business world is crucial to the success of your business. In a crowded and competitive market, it can be challenging to stand out and attract customers. But by differentiating yourself, you can set your business apart from the competition and create a unique value proposition that resonates with your target audience.

So how do you go about differentiating yourself in the business world? Here are a few key strategies to consider:

Identify your unique selling proposition: Your unique selling proposition (USP) is what sets your business apart from the competition. It's important to identify your USP and communicate it clearly and consistently to your target audience. This may involve highlighting a unique feature or benefit of your product or service, or positioning your business as the best choice in a particular market or niche.

Focus on customer experience: Providing an exceptional customer experience is a key way to differentiate your business. This may involve offering top-quality products or services, providing exceptional customer service, or creating a seamless and convenient customer journey. By focusing on the customer experience, you can create loyal and satisfied customers who are more likely to recommend your business to others.

Emphasize your values and mission: Consumers today are increasingly interested in supporting businesses that align with their values and beliefs. By highlighting your values and mission, you can differentiate your business and therefore attract customers who are passionate about the same things as you.

Foster innovation: Innovation is a key driver of differentiation in the business world. By staying up-to-date on industry trends and continuously looking for ways to improve and evolve your products or services, you can differentiate your business and stay ahead of the competition.

Collaborate and network: Collaborating with other businesses and individuals and building strong networks can help to differentiate your business and expand your reach. By forming partnerships and alliances, you can access new markets, resources, and expertise that can help to set your business apart.

By implementing these strategies and differentiating yourself in the business world, you can create a unique and compelling value proposition that attracts and retains customers. With differentiation, you can stand out in a crowded and competitive market and increase the chances of success for your business.

CHAPTER 6

The Power of Value Proposition

"Try not to become a man of success. Rather become a man of value." - Albert Einstein.

Creating a business with value is essential to the success and sustainability of any company. Value can take many forms, including economic value, social value, and personal value. In order to create a business with value, it's important to consider the needs and desires of your target audience, as well as the impact that your business will have on the world.

Economic value refers to the tangible and intangible benefits that a business provides to its customers. This can include the quality and affordability of products or services, as well as the convenience and efficiency of the customer experience. To create economic value, it's important to understand the needs and preferences of your target market, and to offer products or services that meet those needs in a way that is competitively priced and of high quality.

Costco is a retail company that offers a wide range of products, including groceries, household goods, electronics, and more. One of the key ways that Costco offers economic value to its consumers is through its low prices and bulk purchasing options. By buying in bulk and offering products at wholesale prices, the company is able to provide significant savings to its customers.

Social value refers to the positive impact that a business has on the world and the people within it. This can include things like environmental sustainability, philanthropy, and social responsibility. To create social value, it's important to consider the values and beliefs of your target audience, and to then align your business practices with those values. This can involve the likes of sourcing materials ethically, using environmentally friendly practices, and giving back to the community through charitable efforts.

Toms is a company that is known for its commitment to social and environmental responsibility. One of the key ways that the company offers social value to its consumers is through its One for One business model, which donates a pair of shoes to a child in need for every pair purchased. This not only helps to provide children with access to basic necessities, but also helps to create a sense of community and connection between Toms customers and the people they are helping to support. Additionally, Toms offers a range of environmentally sustainable products, which can provide social value to consumers by helping to reduce their environmental impact and support the company's commitment to sustainability.

Personal value refers to the emotional or psychological benefits that a business provides to its customers. This can include things like self-expression, personal growth, and fulfillment. To create personal value, it's important to understand the goals and desires of your target market, and to offer products or services that help customers achieve those goals and fulfill their desires.

A therapy business offers personal value to its clients by providing a safe and confidential space for individuals to explore their thoughts, feelings, and behaviors. Through therapy, individuals can gain a deeper understanding of themselves and the issues that are impacting their lives. They can work to develop coping skills and strategies to better manage their challenges. Therapy can also help individuals to improve their relationships, communicate more effectively, and make positive changes in their lives.

Ultimately, creating a business with value is about understanding the needs and desires of your target audience and offering products or services that meet them in a way that is both meaningful and impactful. By offering value, you can build a loyal customer base and establish a strong reputation in the market.

CHAPTER 7

Identifying Your Ideal Customer

"Everyone is not your customer." - Seth Godin

Identifying your target market is an essential step in the process of brainstorming and developing your business idea. Your target market is the group of consumers that you are targeting with your business, and understanding their needs, preferences, and behaviors is crucial to the success of your business. By identifying your target market, you can tailor your products or services to meet their specific needs and create a unique and compelling value proposition that resonates with them.

So how do you go about identifying your target market? Here are a few key steps to consider:

Define your product or service: The first step is to clearly define your product or service. Consider what you are offering and how it meets the needs or solves the problems of your potential customers.

Research your market: Once you have defined your product or service, it's important to research your market to get a better understanding of your potential customers. This may involve conducting market research, such as surveys or focus groups, or analyzing data on your industry and competitors.

Identify your target audience: Based on your research, it's time to identify your target audience. Consider factors such as age, gender, income, education, location, and interests when determining who your target market is.

Define your target market's needs and preferences: Once you have identified your target audience, it's important to understand their needs and preferences. Consider what motivates them, what challenges they face, and what they are looking for in a product or service.

Segment your market: Depending on the size and complexity of your market, you may want to segment your target audience into smaller, more specific groups. This can help you tailor your marketing efforts and create more targeted and effective messaging.

By following these steps and carefully identifying your target market, you can create a business idea that is tailored to the needs and preferences of your potential customers. This will not only help you to create a unique and compelling value proposition that resonates with your target audience but it will also set your business apart from the competition.

CHAPTER 8

The Importance of Taking Action

"There's no shortage of remarkable ideas, what's missing is the will to execute them." – Seth Godin

In the world of entrepreneurship, it's not enough to simply have a good idea – you also need to be able to execute on that idea. Execution is the process of turning an idea into a reality, and it is an essential part of the entrepreneurial journey. It involves turning your business plan into action, taking the necessary steps to bring your product or service to market, and building a successful company.

Execution is often the most challenging and rewarding part of entrepreneurship. It requires a wide range of skills and knowledge, including business planning, marketing, financial management, and leadership. It also requires persistence, resilience, and adaptability, as you will inevitably face challenges and setbacks along the way.

So how do you go about executing on your business idea? Below are a few ideas to think about:

Develop a clear and actionable plan: Having a clear and actionable plan in place is essential to the success of your business. This includes setting specific and measurable goals, as well as identifying the steps you will take to achieve those goals. It also involves having a timeline in place and holding yourself and your team accountable to meeting deadlines and milestones.

Secure funding: Depending on the nature of your business, you may need to secure funding in order to execute on your business idea. This may involve seeking out investors, applying for grants or loans, or most commonly bootstrapping your business with your personal funds. It's important to carefully research your options and choose the best financing strategy for your business.

Build a team: Building a strong and capable team is crucial to the success of your business. This could mean hiring employees, outsourcing certain tasks, or forming partnerships with other businesses or individuals. It's important to choose team members who are skilled, reliable, and aligned with your business goals and values.

Implement marketing and sales strategies: Marketing and sales are key to bringing your product or service to market and generating revenue. It's important to identify your target market and develop strategies that will effectively reach and engage that audience. This may involve creating a website, social media presence, or marketing materials, as well as developing sales channels and processes.

Be agile and adaptable: As an entrepreneur, you will likely face numerous challenges and setbacks. It's important to be agile and adaptable in order to respond to changing circumstances and pivot when required. Examples include, making changes to your business plan or strategies, or even pivoting to a new business idea altogether.

By following these steps and executing on your business idea in an effective and efficient manner, you can increase the chances of success for your business. It's important to be disciplined, focused, and driven, and to stay true to your vision and values. With persistence and determination, you can turn your business idea into a reality.

CHAPTER 9

Making the Leap: Deciding When to Launch Your Business

"In the end, we only regret the chances we didn't take, relationships we were afraid to have and the decisions we waited too long to make." - Lewis Carroll

Deciding when to start your business is a crucial step in the process of turning your business idea into a reality. While it's important to be passionate and excited about your idea, it's also important to be realistic and consider the timing carefully. Consider the following when deciding when to start your business:

Do you have the necessary resources? Starting a business requires a significant investment of time, money, and energy. It's important to ensure that you have the necessary resources in place to get your business off the ground.This includes financial resources, expertise, and support.

Is the timing right? Consider external factors such as the state of the economy, the competitive landscape, and consumer demand when deciding when to start your business. It may be more advantageous to wait until conditions are more favorable or until you have the resources required to succeed.

Are you ready? Starting a business is a significant undertaking that requires dedication, hard work, and resilience. It's important to be honest with yourself about whether you are ready to take on the challenges and responsibilities of entrepreneurship.

Do you have a plan? A well-developed business plan can help you to clarify your business idea, set goals, and map out a path for success. It's important to have a solid plan in place before starting your business to increase your chances of success.

By considering these factors and being realistic about the resources, timing, and readiness required to start a business, you can make an informed decision about when to turn your business idea into a reality.

Part III: Launch

CHAPTER 10

Crafting a Blueprint for Success

"Plan your work for today and every day, then work your plan." - Margaret Thatcher

The first step to launching a successful business is developing a comprehensive and well-thought-out business plan. This is a document that outlines the key elements of a business, including its products or services, target market, marketing and sales strategies, financial projections, and management structure. It serves as a roadmap for the business and helps guide decision-making and strategic planning.

Developing a business plan requires careful research and analysis, as well as the ability to think critically about the direction you want your business to take. It's important to be as specific and realistic as possible when developing your plan, as this will help you stay focused and on track as you work to launch and grow your business.

There are several key components that should be included in a business plan including the following:

Executive summary: This is a brief overview of the key points of your business plan. It should highlight the main points of your business, including your products or services, target market, and financial projections.

Market analysis: This section should provide a detailed analysis of your target market, including information about their needs and preferences, as well as the competition you will face.

Marketing and sales strategy: Identify the marketing channels you will use to reach your target market and the strategies you will employ to sell your products or services. This should include how you will price your products or services, as well as any promotions or discounts you will offer.

Financial plan: Develop a financial plan that includes detailed financial projections for the first three to five years of your business. This should include projected revenue, expenses, and profitability.

Management structure: Identify the key players in your business, including the leadership team, key employees, and any outside advisors or consultants you will be working with.

Once you have completed your business plan, it's important to review and revise it regularly as your business grows and changes. This will help you stay on track and ensure that you are making progress towards your goals.

Overall, a well-crafted business plan is essential for the success of any business. It helps you define your goals, understand your market, and develop a roadmap for success. By taking the time to research and plan ahead, you can increase your chances of success and set your business up for long-term growth.

CHAPTER 11

Market Research

"Without data, you're just another person with an opinion" - W. Edwards Deming.

Market research is an essential component in the process of launching a business. It helps entrepreneurs understand their target market, identify potential customers, and determine the demand for their products or services. Conducting thorough market research allows business owners to make informed decisions about their strategy, pricing, and marketing efforts.

One of the primary benefits of market research is that it allows business owners to identify the needs and preferences of their target audience. This information is crucial for developing products or services that will be well-received by customers. Without proper market research, business owners may end up offering products or services that do not meet the needs of their target audience, thus leading to poor sales and potentially even the failure of the business.

Market research can also help business owners understand their competitors and the current state of the industry. By analyzing the competition, business owners are able to identify areas where they can differentiate themselves and stand out in the market. They can also use this information to identify potential partnerships and collaborations that can help their business grow.

Another important aspect of market research is the ability to gather data on consumer behavior and trends. This information can be used to inform business decisions and tailor marketing efforts to target the right customers at the right time. By staying up-to-date on industry trends, business owners can anticipate changes in the market and adapt their strategies accordingly.

Finally, market research can also help business owners make informed decisions about pricing and marketing strategies. By understanding the demand for their products or services and the willingness of customers to pay certain prices, you can set prices that are competitive and profitable. Market research can also help business owners determine the most effective marketing channels and tactics for reaching their target audience.

As mentioned, market research is an essential element of launching a business. It helps entrepreneurs understand their target market, identify potential customers, and make informed decisions about their business strategy, pricing, and marketing efforts. By investing the time and effort in market research, business owners can increase their chances of success and set their business up for long-term growth.

CHAPTER 12

Funding Your Dreams

"Don't assume that borrowing lots of money can make your startup fly. There are many things to the business other than investors, and it's possible to succeed with your startup without breaking the bank." - Barnaby Lashbrooke

Starting a business often requires a significant investment of time and money, and financing is a crucial aspect of the process. For many entrepreneurs, the most common source of financing is their own personal savings or assets. This is known as bootstrapping, and it can be a challenging but rewarding way to finance a business.

While bootstrapping allows business owners to retain complete control over their business and avoid taking on debt or giving up equity, it also requires careful planning and resourcefulness. Those who are bootstrapping their businesses may need to be creative in finding ways to minimize costs and generate revenue from the outset.

If personal savings or assets are not sufficient to fully fund a business, there are other financing options that entrepreneurs may consider. One option is a traditional bank loan, which typically requires collateral, such as a personal guarantee or assets, and may have strict repayment terms. Business owners may also be required to provide detailed business plans and financial projections to secure a loan.

Another option is grants, which are financial awards given to businesses, typically by government agencies or non-profit organizations, to support specific projects or initiatives. Grants may be available to businesses in a particular industry or region, or to businesses that meet certain criteria, such as those owned by women or minorities.

Equity financing is another option for businesses seeking funding. With this, business owners sell a portion of their business in exchange for investment. This can be an attractive option for businesses that do not want to take on debt or that are unable to secure a traditional loan.

Finally, business owners may also consider crowdfunding as a way to secure financing . Crowdfunding involves raising small amounts of money from a large number of people, typically through an online platform. This can be a useful way for businesses to test the market for their products or services and raise funds from a large number of potential customers.

In conclusion, financing is a crucial aspect of launching a business. While bootstrapping a business with personal savings or assets can be a challenging but rewarding option, there are also other financing options available. These include traditional loans, grants, equity financing, and crowdfunding. It is important for business owners to carefully consider the terms and conditions of any financing agreement and choose the option that is most appropriate for their own business needs.

CHAPTER 13

Legal Structure

"In the end, you have to protect yourself at all times." - Floyd Mayweather, Jr.

Choosing the right legal structure for a business is an important decision that can have significant consequences for the owner or owners. The legal structure of a business determines how it will be taxed, how it will be managed, and the level of personal liability that the owner or owners will have. There are several different legal structures to choose from, each with its own advantages and disadvantages.

One common legal structure for small businesses is a sole proprietorship. A sole proprietorship is owned and operated by a single individual, and the owner is personally responsible for all debts and liabilities of the business. This legal structure is relatively simple and inexpensive to set up, but it also provides the owner with no liability protection.

Another option is a partnership, which involves two or more individuals working together to run a business.

Partnerships can either be general partnerships or limited partnerships. In a general partnership, all partners are personally liable for the debts and liabilities of the business, while in a limited partnership, only some partners are personally liable. Partnerships offer the advantage of shared ownership and management, but they also involve a higher level of personal risk for the partners.

A corporation is a separate legal entity owned by shareholders who elect a board of directors to manage the business. Corporations offer the advantage of limited liability protection for the owners, as the shareholders are not personally responsible for the debts and liabilities of the business. However, corporations also involve a higher level of complexity and expense to set up and operate, and they are subject to more stringent regulatory requirements.

Finally, a limited liability company (LLC) is a legal structure that combines elements of both a corporation and a partnership. Like a corporation, an LLC provides limited liability protection for the owners, but like a partnership, it allows for flexibility in management and taxation. LLCs are a popular choice for small businesses because they offer the benefits of both corporations and partnerships without the drawbacks of either.

When choosing a legal structure for a business, it is important to consider a variety of factors, including the size and scope of the business, the level of personal risk that the owner or owners are willing to take on, and the potential tax implications. It is also a good idea to seek the advice of a lawyer or other legal professional to ensure that the chosen legal structure is an appropriate one.

Choosing the right legal structure is an important decision that can have significant consequences. By considering the size and scope of the business, the level of personal risk, and the potential tax implications, business owners can choose a legal structure that is appropriate for their needs.

CHAPTER 14

Building a Strong Brand Identity

"Your brand is the single most important investment you can make in your business." - Steve Forbes

Branding is an essential aspect of launching a business. It involves creating a unique identity and image for a business that distinguishes it from its competitors and helps it stand out in the market. A strong brand can help a business establish credibility, build customer loyalty, and drive sales.

Customers are more likely to do business with a company that they know and trust, and a strong brand can help establish that trust. By consistently delivering on its brand promises, a business can build a reputation for quality and reliability, which can lead to increased customer loyalty and sales.

Branding is also an important tool for attracting and retaining customers. A strong brand can help a business stand out in a crowded market and grab the attention of potential customers. By creating a memorable and distinctive brand, a business can create a lasting impression on customers and make them more likely to choose its products or services over those of its competitors.

Finally, branding can help businesses increase their value. A strong brand can make a business more attractive to potential partners, investors, and employees, which can help it grow and expand. A well-known and respected brand can also increase the value of a business, making it more valuable when the time comes to sell.

In conclusion, branding is an essential aspect of launching a business. It helps businesses create a consistent image and message, build trust and credibility with customers, attract and retain customers, and increase their value. By investing in branding, businesses can set themselves up for long-term success and growth.

CHAPTER 15

Getting the Word Out

"Marketing is not a function, it is the whole business seen from the customer's point of view." - Peter F. Drucker

Marketing is the process of identifying and reaching potential customers, as well as promoting and selling products or services. It is an essential aspect of launching a business, as it helps businesses establish themselves in the market and reach their target audience. There are a variety of different marketing tactics and strategies that can be used to effectively market products or services.

One of the primary benefits of marketing a business is that it helps establish brand awareness. By effectively promoting their products or services, businesses can generate interest and build a reputation for quality and reliability. This is especially important in a crowded market, where it can be difficult for businesses to stand out and differentiate themselves from their competitors.

Another benefit of marketing a business is that it helps to attract and retain customers. By consistently promoting their products or services and providing value to customers, businesses can build relationships with them and increase the likelihood of repeat business. Marketing is also an important tool for attracting new customers, as it helps businesses reach and engage with potential customers who may not have otherwise been aware of their products or services.

There are a variety of different marketing tactics that businesses can use to effectively market their products or services. These include advertising, public relations, content marketing, and social media marketing. Each of these tactics has its own advantages and disadvantages, and it is important for businesses to carefully consider which tactics will be most effective for their target audience and goals.

CHAPTER 16

The Customer is Always Right

"Right or wrong, the customer is always right." -
Harry Gordon Selfridge

Customer service is the process of assisting and satisfying customers' needs and expectations. It is a key aspect of any business, as it helps to build customer loyalty and drive sales. The saying "the customer is always right" is a well-known phrase that isn't always true but emphasizes the importance of customer service and the need to prioritize the needs and satisfaction of customers.

One of the primary benefits of good customer service is that it helps to build customer loyalty. Customers are more likely to do business with a company that they know and trust, and providing excellent customer service is a key way to establish that trust. By consistently delivering on their brand promises and meeting the needs of customers, businesses can create a positive reputation and encourage customers to return and recommend their products or services to others.

Another benefit of good customer service is that it can help businesses to identify and address issues and challenges. By actively listening to and engaging with customers, businesses can gather valuable feedback and insights into the customer experience. This can help to identify areas for improvement and make necessary changes to better meet the needs of customers.

"Under promise, over deliver" is one of my favorite customer service strategies that involves setting expectations that are slightly lower than what you are actually capable of achieving, and then consistently exceeding those expectations. This approach can be highly effective in building trust and loyalty with your customers. When a customer feels like they are getting more than they expected, they are likely to feel satisfied and valued, which can lead to repeat business and positive word-of-mouth. This strategy can be particularly useful in situations where you are unable to meet a customer's initial request or expectations, as it allows you to mitigate disappointment and turn a potentially negative experience into a positive one.

Over the top customer service can also help businesses to increase sales and revenue. By providing a positive and satisfying customer experience, businesses can encourage customers to make repeat purchases and recommend their products or services to others. This can help businesses to drive growth and increase their market share.

Understanding the importance of customer service is essential for the success of any business. Providing excellent customer service helps to build customer loyalty, identify and address issues and challenges, and increase sales and revenue. By prioritizing the needs and satisfaction of customers, businesses can set themselves up for long-term success and growth.

CHAPTER 17

Staying Ahead of the Game

"Creativity is thinking up new things. Innovation is doing new things." - Theodore Levitt.

Innovation is a crucial component of any successful business, and it is especially important when launching a new venture. By constantly seeking out new and innovative ways to improve your products or services, you can stay ahead of the competition and position your business for long-term success.

One of the key ways to foster innovation is to create a culture that encourages and rewards creative thinking. This can involve setting aside dedicated time for employees to brainstorm and come up with new ideas, or offering incentives for employees who come up with successful innovations. It is also important to create an environment where employees feel comfortable sharing their ideas and are not afraid of failure.

Another important aspect of innovation is staying up to date on industry trends and developments. This can involve attending conferences and trade shows, reading industry publications, and keeping an eye on what your competitors are doing. By staying informed, you can identify new opportunities for innovation and be among the first to introduce new products or services to the market.

In addition to staying current, it is also important to always be looking for ways to improve and evolve your business. This can involve continuously fine-tuning your products or services to meet the changing needs of your customers, or exploring new markets and partnerships that can help you grow. By staying agile and open to change, you can ensure that your business stays relevant and competitive.

Ultimately, innovation is essential for any business looking to succeed in today's fast-paced, constantly changing market. By creating a culture of innovation, staying up to date on industry trends, and always looking for ways to improve and evolve, you can ensure that your business stays ahead of the game and positions itself for long-term success.

Part IV: Scale

CHAPTER 18

Foundation

"Think big, start small, then scale or fail fast." –
Mats Lederhausen

Once you have the foundation of your business in place, it's natural to start thinking about how to scale and grow. However, before you start scaling, it's important to make sure that you have a solid business model and proof of concept. Scaling can be costly and time-consuming, and it's important to ensure that you have a solid foundation before you invest too much time and resources into doing so.

A solid business model is essential for any successful business, and it's important to spend time developing and refining your model before you start scaling. This may involve identifying your target market, developing a marketing plan, and identifying your unique value proposition. It's also important to conduct market research to ensure that there is a demand for your product or service.

In addition to a solid business model, it's also important to have proof of concept before you start scaling. This means that you need to test and validate your business idea to ensure that it is viable and has the potential to be scaled. This could mean conducting small-scale pilot tests, gathering feedback from potential customers, and refining your product or service based on this feedback.

An example I always fall back on of a business that might be tough to scale is selling candy out of your locker. It might seem like a fun and easy way to make some extra money, but it can be a tough business model to scale. One of the main challenges of scaling a business that relies on selling candy out of a locker is the limited customer base. Your customer base is essentially limited to the students and faculty at your school, which may not be a large enough market to support significant growth. Additionally, there may be competition from other students who are also selling candy out of their lockers, which can make it difficult to stand out and attract a significant customer base.

Overall, it's important to take the time to build a solid foundation for your business before you start scaling. This will help to ensure that you have a strong foundation to build upon as you grow, and it will also help you avoid costly mistakes that could derail your growth efforts.

CHAPTER 19

Automate Some Processes

"The first rule of any technology used in a business is that automation applied to an efficient operation will magnify the efficiency. The second is that automation applied to an inefficient operation will magnify the inefficiency." – Bill Gates

Automation is a key element to consider when looking for ways to scale your business. Looking back on my teenage entrepreneurial endeavors, my biggest regret is not taking advantage of the opportunity to automate certain aspects of my businesses. Automating certain processes and tasks can help you increase efficiency, reduce costs, and free up time and resources that can be better spent on other areas of the business.

There are many different ways that automation can be used to scale a business. For example, you can use automation to streamline your marketing efforts, such as by using tools that help you automate email campaigns and social media posts. You can also use it to improve your customer service, by using chatbots or automated systems to handle routine inquiries and tasks.

In addition to these examples, there are many other ways that automation can be used to scale a business. The key is to identify the areas of your business that are most suitable for automation, and to carefully consider the costs and benefits of implementing automated systems.

When implementing automation, it's important to keep in mind that it's not always a one-size-fits-all solution. Different businesses will have different needs, and it's important to customize your automation efforts to meet the specific needs of your business. For example, you may need to invest in specialized software or hire staff with expertise in automation in order to effectively implement these systems.

All in all, learning how to automate certain processes and be more efficient is a great way to scale your business. By carefully considering the costs and benefits of automation, and customizing your efforts to meet the specific needs of your business, you can effectively use it to help your business grow and succeed.

CHAPTER 20

Hire Wisely

"When people are financially invested, they want a return. When people are emotionally invested, they want to contribute." - Simon Sinek

Hiring employees is an important step in scaling your business, as it allows you to bring on additional help and take on more work as you grow. However, hiring employees also brings with it a number of considerations and challenges that you need to be aware of.

Remember, hiring doesn't always mean bringing on full-time employees or paying six-figure salaries. There are a variety of options available for getting additional help as you scale your business, including hiring contractors and virtual assistants.

If you are not familiar with a virtual assistant (often referred to as a "VA"), it's essentially exactly what it sounds like. VA's are virtual contractors who provide a handful of different services remotely, usually over the internet. Hiring virtual assistants can be a cost-effective way to scale your business, as you can often find highly skilled professionals at a lower cost than you would pay for comparable talent in your own country.

One of the key considerations when hiring employees is finding the right people for the job. This means taking the time to carefully assess your needs, create detailed job descriptions, and then actively seek out candidates who are a good fit for your business. This may involve using job boards, advertising on social media, or working with a recruiting agency.

Once you've identified potential candidates, it's important to thoroughly vet them to ensure that they are the right fit for your business. This may involve conducting in-depth interviews, checking references, and requiring applicants to complete relevant tests or assessments.

In addition to finding the right people, it's also important to have a clear plan in place for onboarding and training new hires. This should include providing them with the tools and resources they need to succeed in their roles, as well as setting clear goals and expectations.

Finally, as you scale your business and bring on more employees, it's important to stay compliant with employment laws and regulations. This may include issues such as payroll, benefits, and workplace safety. Working with an HR professional or consulting with a lawyer can help ensure that you are in compliance with all relevant laws and regulations.

Hiring employees is an important step in scaling your business, but it requires careful planning and attention to detail. By taking the time to find the right people and put systems in place to support them, you can effectively scale your business and achieve your growth goals.

CHAPTER 21

Innovate

"Innovation is the unrelenting drive to break the status quo and develop anew where few have dared to go." - Steven Jeffes

Innovation is a key component of any successful business, and it's especially important when it comes to scaling. By constantly seeking out new and creative ways to solve problems and meet the needs of your customers, you can position your business for long-term growth and success.

There are a number of ways that you can approach innovation as you scale your business. One approach is to constantly seek out new opportunities and ideas, whether through market research, customer feedback, or industry trends. This can help you stay ahead of the curve and identify new areas for growth.

Another approach is to encourage a culture of innovation within your organization. This can involve fostering a sense of openness and collaboration, and encouraging employees to share their ideas and take risks. You can also consider implementing processes and systems that support innovation, such as design thinking or agile development methodologies.

It's also important to be willing to take risks and try new things as you scale your business. This may involve introducing new products or services, entering new markets, or experimenting with new business models. By being open to change and willing to take calculated risks, you can create opportunities for growth and success.

Overall, innovating is an important part of scaling your business. By constantly seeking out new ideas and being open to change, you can position your business for long-term growth and success.

CHAPTER 22

Customer Connection

"There is only one boss. The customer. And he can fire everybody in the company from the chairman on down, simply by spending his money somewhere else." - Sam Walton

As you scale your business, it's essential to maintain a strong connection with your customers. Loyal customers are the foundation of any successful business, and building a strong relationship with them is critical for long-term success. Here are some key strategies for connecting with your customers as you scale your business:

Empathy: Demonstrating empathy and understanding for your customers' needs and concerns is a key aspect of building strong relationships. This may involve actively listening to your customers, asking for their feedback, and taking their needs into account as you make decisions about your business.

Respect: Treating your customers with dignity and respect, and valuing their input and feedback, is another important aspect of building a positive relationship. By demonstrating respect for your customers, you can build trust and create a positive experience for them.

Client-centered practices: As you scale your business, it's important to build client-centered practices into every aspect of your business. This means ensuring that every member of your team demonstrates empathy, respect, and open-mindedness internally, so that a collaborative culture of innovation can emerge.

Rapport-building: Empowering your team to build rapport with your clients and create connections is essential for building strong relationships with your customers. This can help your product sell itself and create raving fans of your business.

Overall, connecting with your customers is essential for the success of your business, and it's especially important when it comes to scaling your business. By getting to know your customer, you can create strong relationships with the people that keep your business afloat and set the foundation for long-term success.

CHAPTER 23

Study Industry Leaders

"Be passionate and bold. Always keep learning. You stop doing useful things if you don't learn. So the last part to me is the key, especially if you have had some initial success. It becomes even more critical that you have the learning 'bit' always switched on."
- Satya Nadella

If you are ready to scale, there is no better way to learn how to scale than studying those who have done it themselves. Studying industry leaders can be a valuable way to learn about successful strategies for scaling a business. By examining the approaches taken by successful business leaders, you can gain insight into what works and what doesn't, and apply those lessons to your own efforts to scale your business.

For instance, consider these 5 entrepreneurs:

Elon Musk: Musk is the CEO of SpaceX and Tesla, both of which have experienced significant growth in recent years. One of the keys to Musk's success has been his ability to identify and pursue ambitious goals, such as developing reusable rockets and creating electric vehicles with a long range. He has also been willing to take calculated risks and make bold decisions, such as investing in advanced manufacturing technologies and acquiring other companies to accelerate growth.

Oprah Winfrey: Winfrey is best known for her successful talk show, but she has also built a media empire through her production company, Harpo Productions, and her ownership of the Oprah Winfrey Network. One of the keys to Winfrey's success has been her ability to connect with her audience and build a loyal following. She has also been effective at diversifying her portfolio, investing in a range of ventures including magazines, books, and television programs.

Jeff Bezos: Bezos is the founder of Amazon, which has become one of the world's largest online retailers. One of the keys to Amazon's success has been its focus on customer satisfaction, including offering a wide selection of products, fast shipping, and a user-friendly website. Bezos has also been willing to embrace new technologies and diversify the company's offerings, including expanding into areas such as cloud computing and streaming media.

Steve Jobs: Jobs co-founded Apple and played a key role in the company's success as a pioneer in the personal computer industry. Jobs was known for his attention to design and his ability to anticipate consumer needs, as well as his expertise in assembling and leading talented teams. He was also willing to take risks, such as introducing new products and technologies that were ahead of their time.

Mark Zuckerberg: Zuckerberg is the co-founder and CEO of Facebook, which has become one of the world's most popular social media platforms. One of the keys to Facebook's success has been its ability to constantly evolve and adapt to changing consumer needs, as well as its focus on building a strong community of users. Zuckerberg has also been effective at acquiring other companies and incorporating their technologies into the Facebook platform to drive growth.

Studying industry leaders can be a valuable way to learn about successful strategies for scaling a business. By examining the approaches taken by successful business leaders, you can gain insight into what works and what doesn't, and apply those lessons to your own efforts when scaling your business.

Part V: Summary

CHAPTER 24

Closing Thoughts

If you've made it this far, it's clear that you are determined and I admire that. When I was your age, I struggled to even get through a chapter of a book. Now that you have all the resources and education that I could only dream of having at your age, it is up to you to put it into action.

Whenever I speak with aspiring business men and women, I always emphasize the importance of execution. From my experience in the entrepreneurship space, I have noticed that a common problem is having lots of ideas but never taking the necessary steps to make them a reality. As Gary Vaynerchuk once said, "Your ideas may be solid or even good...but you have to actually execute on them for them to matter."

With that being said, I encourage you to go out there and make it happen. Remember that having great ideas is just the starting point, it's the execution that will make them a reality.

Sincerely,

Brendan Cox

Made in the USA
Monee, IL
04 June 2023